EDGE BOOKS™

THE WORLD'S TOP TENS

# THE WORLD'S DEADLIEST SHARKS

by Nick Healy

Consultant:
Debbie Nuzzolo
Education Manager
Sea World, San Diego, California

Capstone press
Mankato, Minnesota

Edge Books are published by Capstone Press,
151 Good Counsel Drive, P.O. Box 669, Mankato, Minnesota, 56002.
www.capstonepress.com

Library of Congress Cataloging-in-Publication Data
Healy, Nick.
The world's deadliest sharks / Nick Healy.
    p. cm.—(Edge Books. The world's top tens)
    Summary:"Describes in countdown format 10 of the world's most dangerous sharks"
–Provided by publisher.
    Includes bibliographical references and index.
    ISBN-13: 978-0-7368-5453-5 (hardcover)
    ISBN-10: 0-7368-5453-3 (hardcover)
    1. Shark attacks—Juvenile literature. 2. Sharks—Juvenile literature. I. Title. II. Series:
    Edge Books. World's top tens (Mankato, Minn.)
QL638.93.H43 2006
597.3—dc22
                                                                    2005020097

**Editorial Credits**
Mandy Marx, editor; Kate Opseth, set designer; Jenny Bergstrom, book designer;
    Kelly Garvin, photo researcher/photo editor


**Photo Credits**
Corbis/Kirk Aeder/Icon SMI, 21; Paul A. Souders, 29
Getty Images Inc./Russell Shakespeare/Newspix, 11
Jeff Rotman, 10, 25, 26 (bottom left)
National Archives and Records Administration, 19
Peter Arnold, Inc./Klaus Jost, 24
Seapics/C & M Fallows, 22, 27 (bottom left); James D. Watt, cover, 16, 27
    (top right); Kike Calvo, 4, 27 (bottom right); Manfred Bail, 6, 26 (top left);
    Mark Conlin, 20, 27 (middle right); Masa Ushioda, 18, 27 (middle left);
    Michael S. Nolan, 15, 27 (top left); Nat Sumanatemeya, 9, 26 (top right);
    Richard Herrmann, 12, 26 (bottom right)

1  2  3  4  5  6  11  10  09  08  07  06

# TABLE OF CONTENTS

# DEADLY SHARKS

Sharks attack their prey with ferocious strength and astonishing speed.

Sharks are killing machines. Their powerful bodies are shaped like torpedoes. Their dorsal, or back, fins slice the surface of the water. Their eyes stare coldly ahead. And their open jaws display mouthfuls of razor sharp teeth.

A shark's teeth are a fright to behold. Whether they are long, triangular, or hook-shaped, shark teeth grow row upon row. New teeth are always ready to pop up, replacing those ripped out during attacks.

Of the more than 350 species of sharks, only about 30 are dangerous to people. Although most sharks are harmless to humans, dozens of shark attacks occur each year. And each year, a handful of victims die from those attacks. Which sharks should you watch out for? Read on to find out.

# 10

Scuba divers take their chances when they swim near gray reef sharks.

HABITAT: Central and western Pacific Ocean and the Indian Ocean ·

SIZE: 6.5 to 8 feet (2 to 2.4 meters)

HABITS: Gray reef sharks hunt along the outer edge of reefs and in lagoons.

# GRAY REEF SHARK

Gray reef sharks lurk at the edge of coral reefs. These sharks are a common sight to scuba divers and fishers. In fact, gray reef sharks are known to be curious about people. They often swim up for a closer look. That's when trouble begins.

Gray reef sharks become aggressive if they feel trapped. They arch their backs and grind their teeth. Their pectoral, or side, fins lower as they turn up their noses. Gray reef sharks thrash about in circles before they attack.

These sharks often attack spear fishers. In these cases, a spear fisher's catch drips blood into the water. That blood attracts gray reef sharks. Attacks usually don't last long, but they are violent and bloody. These sharks often deliver several quick bites before swimming off.

# 9 BLACKTIP SHARK

Blacktip sharks are very dangerous, especially if you're a sardine. Blacktips feed on fish that move in large schools, like sardines and anchovies.

For blacktips, mealtime is a feeding frenzy. They attack from below, snatching prey as they plow through schools of fish. Finally, blacktips blast through the surface of the water. They twist in midair and splash back down.

Blacktips have been known to attack humans without cause, especially surfers. In Florida, blacktips are blamed for one of every five shark attacks. The sharks probably mistake surfers for other animals. But for surfers, this can be a very painful case of mistaken identity.

Blacktips prowl tropical waters looking for a tasty meal.

HABITAT: Warm waters, especially near the equator

SIZE: Up to 6.5 feet (2 meters) in length

FEATURES: Long, pointed snouts and black markings along the edges of their fins

# 8 SAND TIGER SHARK

The sand tiger shark's hook-shaped teeth and beady eyes give it a terrifying appearance.

Sand tiger sharks often swim with their jaws open. They display rows of jagged teeth. These sharks have been labeled man-eaters because of their frightening appearance.

Surprisingly, sand tigers are usually harmless. But their mood can change quickly. These sharks respond violently when bothered. They have attacked dozens of people. In at least two attacks, the victims were killed.

This man survived a sand tiger shark attack. He was lucky not to lose his leg.

FEATURES: Bulky bodies and flat, pointed snouts

TEETH: 48 upper teeth and 46 lower teeth

TYPES: Four species of sand tigers live in the Atlantic, Pacific, and Indian oceans.

# 7

With its striking appearance, it is no wonder the shortfin mako is considered a trophy to fishers.

# SHORTFIN MAKO SHARK

**S**hortfin makos are the fastest fish in the sea. Their pointed snouts slice through the water at 25 miles (40 kilometers) per hour.

Fishers prize a catch like the shortfin mako. Those who hook this shark get a good fight. When hooked, makos swim away at high speeds. They jump and turn somersaults. Makos have even leapt inside boats and charged people.

Divers also see scary things when these sharks come around. Makos trap prey, and people, by swimming figure eights around them. They dart past with mouths open and teeth bared. When they attack, they attack quickly. Makos have been blamed for several human deaths and many more injuries.

**HABITAT:** Warm waters around the world

**SIZE:** Up to 13 feet (3.9 meters) long and weighing up to 1,200 pounds (544.3 kilograms)

**FYI:** Fishing has reduced the number of shortfin makos and threatens the species.

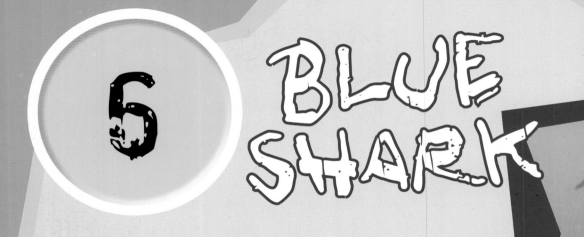

# 6 BLUE SHARK

Blue sharks look like the sharp blade of a sword. And they are just as deadly. Their backs are deep blue, and their bellies are bright white. The blue shark's eyes are huge and black.

These sharks swim in packs. They usually do not come into contact with humans. But when they do, results can be tragic.

Blue sharks trap their victims by swimming circles around them. In order to get away, a person has to risk being attacked. In such cases, the sharks often take only a test bite. Luckily, blue sharks usually don't like the taste of human flesh. But even a nibble means a bloody mess for the victim.

Blue sharks swim in packs of either all male or all female sharks.

**HABITAT:** Oceans worldwide, in warm and cold waters

**SIZE:** 8 to 12.5 feet (2.4 to 3.8 meters) long

**HABITS:** They usually stay near the surface but have been seen as deep as 500 feet (152.4 meters).

**5**

The strange shape of this shark's snout helps it steer through the water.

HABITAT: Oceans around the world, often near coral reefs

PREY: Fish and squid

SIZE: Up to 20 feet (6.1 meters) long

# GREAT HAMMERHEAD SHARK

The hammerhead shark is one of the strangest looking fish in the sea. From the bottom, it looks like a mallet laid on its side. At each end of the mallet sits one eye and one nostril.

Hammerheads have big appetites. They prowl the ocean with their mouths open, catching small prey as they go. For larger meals, hammerheads hunt stingrays and other sharks. They will even eat smaller hammerheads.

Hammerheads swim in shallow waters. But so do swimmers, surfers, and divers. Even the strongest human is no match for the powerful hammerhead.

**4**

# OCEANIC WHITE TIP SHARK

White tips are curious sharks. They swim in deep waters far from humans. But in the case of a shipwreck, they arrive quickly. These sharks swim near to investigate and often take a nibble.

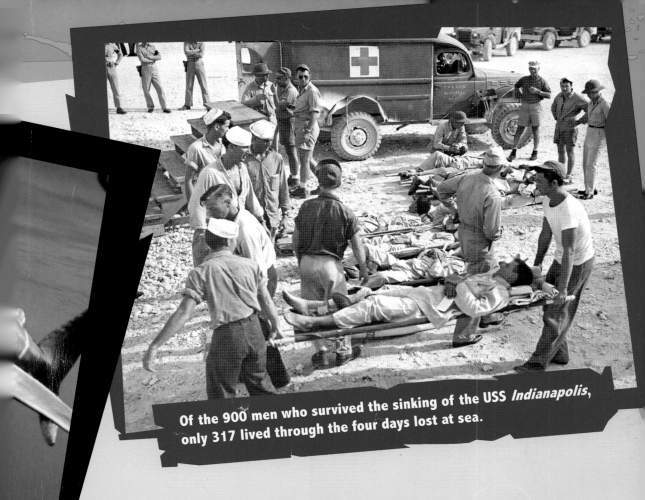

Of the 900 men who survived the sinking of the USS *Indianapolis*, only 317 lived through the four days lost at sea.

In 1945, the USS *Indianapolis* was attacked by the Japanese. The large ship sank into the Pacific Ocean. Hundreds of sailors leapt into the water. Rescuers didn't find them until 4 days later. By then, many survivors of the sinking had been killed by oceanic white tip sharks.

**SIZE:** Up to 13 feet (4 meters) long

**FEATURES:** Long pectoral fins that are rounded and colored white at the end

**COLOR:** Bronze or olive

# 3

# TIGER SHARK

A tiger shark's jaws are strong enough to crack a turtle shell.

Tiger sharks were named for their distinct markings. And just like the big cats, these sharks are skilled hunters. They hunt in packs and often tear prey apart in a group effort.

Tiger sharks live in tropical waters and often travel into shallow lagoons. It is here where they run into humans.

A tiger shark is blamed for attacking Bethany Hamilton, a Hawaiian surfer. She was on her way to becoming a champion surfer when a tiger shark tore off her left arm.

Losing her arm to a tiger shark doesn't stop Bethany Hamilton from surfing.

HABITAT: Indian, Pacific, and Atlantic coasts

SIZE: 15 to 25 feet (4.6 to 7.6 meters) long

FYI: Tiger sharks lose their color and their stripes as they grow older.

21

**2**

Bull sharks are the only sharks with the ability to live in salt water and freshwater.

SIZE: 10 feet (3 meters) long

TEETH: Broad and triangular with rough edges, like a saw blade

FYI: Some experts say the bull shark is the most dangerous shark of all.

# BULL SHARK

**M**ost fish thrive in salt water or freshwater. Bull sharks have the unusual ability to live in both. They lurk in the shallow water along coastlines. From there, these sharks often swim upstream into rivers.

In 2005, bull sharks were to blame for at least two attacks in the Gulf of Mexico. One of them occurred in waist-deep water.

Bull sharks can travel far upstream in rivers. They even swim into connected lakes. Bull sharks are blamed for a series of attacks in New Jersey in 1916. Within 12 days, five people were attacked and four died. Three attacks occurred in an inland creek. The creek was 15 miles (24 kilometers) from open sea.

# GREAT WHITE SHARK

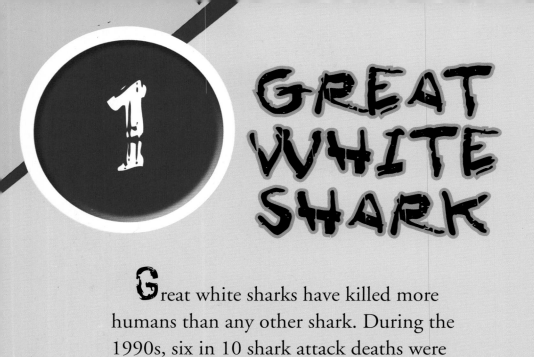

**G**reat white sharks have killed more humans than any other shark. During the 1990s, six in 10 shark attack deaths were caused by great whites.

Great whites' teeth have ragged edges like a steak knife.

Great white sharks are the largest meat-eating shark in the ocean.

Great white attacks are some of the most disturbing. Stories have been told of great white sharks biting people completely in half. A great white captured near Italy had the remains of three people in its stomach.

Great whites probably mistake swimmers for a tasty meal, like a seal. But for the unlucky swimmer, it is a deadly mistake.

**FEATURES:** Blue-gray skin on their backs and tall dorsal fins

**HABITS:** Swim near the surface along coastlines and reefs looking for food

**LIFESPAN:** About 40 years

**SIZE:** Can grow more than 20 feet (6.1 meters) long and weigh more than 6,000 pounds (2,722 kilograms)

25

# The World's DEADLIEST SHARKS

**10**

GRAY REEF SHARK

**9**

BLACKTIP SHARK

SAND TIGER SHARK

**8**

**7**

SHORTFIN MAKO SHARK

BLUE SHARK

6

5

HAMMERHEAD SHARK

OCEANIC WHITE TIP SHARK

3

4

TIGER SHARK

GREAT WHITE SHARK

2

1

BULL SHARK

27

# UNDERSTANDING SHARKS

**S**hark attacks are certainly brutal. But sharks actually pose a very small risk to humans. Each year, more people die from lightning strikes than are killed by sharks. Harmful dog bites are much more common than shark bites. Insects kill more humans each day than sharks do in a year.

On the other hand, people kill more than 30 million sharks each year. As a result, the populations of many shark species are shrinking.

While sharks are dangerous to humans, they are also important to the food chain. Sharks clear the oceans of animals that are weak or old. Their feeding habits help keep the oceans healthy.

Shark attacks remind us that the ocean is their home, and we must respect them. In the end, if we want to use the water, we must share it with the sharks.

At the Sydney Aquarium in Australia, visitors can watch sharks swim right above their heads.

# GLOSSARY

**dorsal fin** (DOR-suhl FIN)—the fin that sticks up from the middle of a shark's back

**lagoon** (luh-GOON)—a shallow pool of seawater separated from the sea by a narrow strip of land

**pectoral fin** (PEK-tor-uhl FIN)—the hard, flat limb on either side of a shark

**prey** (PRAY)—an animal hunted by another animal for food

**reef** (REEF)—an underwater strip of rocks, coral, or sand near the surface of the ocean

**scuba** (SKOO-buh)—self-contained underwater breathing apparatus; divers use scuba equipment to breathe underwater.

**species** (SPEE-sheez)—a group of plants or animals that share common characteristics

# READ MORE

**Betz, Adrienne, and the editors of Time for Kids.** *Sharks!* Time for Kids Science Scoops. New York: HarperTrophy, 2005.

**Lewin, Ted.** *Tooth and Claw: Animal Adventures in the Wild.* New York: HarperCollins, 2003.

**Spilsbury, Richard.** *Great White Shark: In Danger of Extinction!* Animals Under Threat. Chicago: Heinemann Library, 2004.

**Wlodarski, Loran.** *Sharks! From Fear to Fascination.* Orlando: SeaWorld, Inc., 2005.

# INTERNET SITES

FactHound offers a safe, fun way to find Internet sites related to this book. All of the sites on FactHound have been researched by our staff.

Here's how:

1. Visit *www.facthound.com*
2. Type in this special code **0736854533** for age-appropriate sites. Or enter a search word related to this book for a more general search.
3. Click on the **Fetch It** button.

FactHound will fetch the best sites for you!

# Index